1 MONTH OF
FREE
READING

at

www.ForgottenBooks.com

By purchasing this book you are eligible for one month membership to ForgottenBooks.com, giving you unlimited access to our entire collection of over 1,000,000 titles via our web site and mobile apps.

To claim your free month visit:

www.forgottenbooks.com/free482416

ISBN 978-0-483-59053-3
PIBN 10482416

THE MAGI ON THE WAY TO BETHLEHEM.

From a painting by J. Portaels.

Helps Upward

By

Wayland Hoyt, D. D.

United Society of Christian Endeavor
Boston and Chicago

Helps Upward

By
Wayland Hoyt, D. D.

United Society of Christian Endeavor
Boston and Chicago

Copyright, 1899

BY THE

UNITED SOCIETY OF CHRISTIAN ENDEAVOR

Colonial Press:
Electrotyped and Printed by
C. H. Simonds & Co.
Boston, Mass., U. S. A.

CONTENTS.

————•————

HELPS UPWARD.

I.

THE STORY OF AN ANCIENT MARTYRDOM.

SHE was only twenty-two. Her husband had lately died. Her little babe was clinging to her breast. Her mother was a Christian, but her aged father was still a pagan. It was during the persecution under the insane Roman emperor Caracalla. And among others at Carthage, where she lived, the fair and youthful Perpetua was arrested for the crime of being a Christian.

His daughter Perpetua was very dear to her still pagan father; and to him the disgrace of her arrest, and for such a cause, seemed terrible. He visited her prison to plead with her.

"While we were in the hands of the perse-

cutors," Perpetua writes, " my father sought
with all his power to turn me away from the
faith.

" ' Father,' said I, ' do you see this little pitcher
lying here ? '

" He said, ' I see it.'

" Then I said, ' Can it be called by any other
name than what it is ? '

" He answered, ' No.'

" ' Neither can I,' I replied, ' call myself anything else but what I am, — a Christian.' "

She was thrown into a deeper dungeon. " I
was tempted," she said, " for I had never been
in such darkness before.   O what a dreadful
day !   The excessive heat occasioned by the
multitude of prisoners, the rough treatment we
experienced from the soldiers, and, finally, anxi-
ety for my child made me miserable."   Christian
friends managed to procure for her a slightly
more lenient imprisonment, and for a little her
babe was given her.   " The dungeon," said she,
" became a palace to me."

She was soon to meet her public and formal
trial.   Again her father sought to shake her
faith and resolution.

" My daughter," he pleaded, " pity my gray
hairs ; pity thy father ; look upon thy son, who,
if thou diest, cannot long survive."   And, throw-

ing himself at his daughter's feet, he kissed her hands, and drenched them with his tears.

"What shall happen when I come before the tribunal depends on the will of God; for know, we stand not in our own strength, but only by the power of God." It was thus tenderly and yet resolutely that she met the bewailings and beseechings of her father.

At last the day of formal trial came, and she stood before the procurator. There stood again her aged father, if he might, in the last moment, dissolve by tears and pleadings the firmness of her faith.

Said the procurator to Perpetua: "Have pity on thy father's gray hairs; have pity on thy helpless child. Offer sacrifice for the welfare of the emperor."

Answered Perpetua, "That I cannot do."

"Art thou a Christian?" judicially asked the procurator.

"Yes, I am a Christian," was the unwavering answer of the young and tried — yet, to the last, faithful — soul.

"Then," says Perpetua, "the procurator delivered judgment, condemning us to be exposed to the wild beasts. And with hearts full of joy, we returned to our dungeon."

Singing, she entered the arena, and was gored

by the wild cattle; and when that did not finish her, the sword-stroke of the gladiator gave her pure, strong spirit liberty at last.

It is good for us to look, now and then, upon such pictures of that heroic time.

For one thing, it ought to shame us. How constantly we are saying to ourselves, "In my circumstances it is so difficult to be and to live as a Christian ought"! And we make all manner of excuses to ourselves, and lay a ponderous blame on circumstances, and try to make ourselves think that we, at least, whom such iron and hostile circumstances surround, may be excused from brave confession, and high and strenuous endeavor. But our circumstances, how hard soever they may be, are cushions of pleasantness compared with those that closed about such a fair, tender, shrinking woman as was Perpetua. Surely, if she could be so true and strong in her circumstances, we ought to be in ours. How Perpetua, in her beautiful and sweet resisting, ought to shame our kid-glove and slippered, and, too often, whining, Christianity!

Another thing that a vision of such strenuous ancient sainthood will reveal to us is our resource, — our resource for our time and trial, as much as hers for hers. "And with hearts full of joy we returned to our dungeon." The joy of the good was the reason and the resource of Perpetua's strength. And we may have her joy, and so her strength, in her way, — in the only way for all times and for all trials; namely, the way of supreme devotion to our Lord Christ.

What joy, and so what strength; what mastery of circumstances, what inner wealth, outshining all the gauds and glories of the world, will not come to us from a genuinely supreme devotion to Jesus Christ!

Here is another snatch of vision of that ancient suffering, yet triumphing, sainthood. It is an epitaph in the Catacombs. I do not know anything in literature so exquisite. Robert Browning tells it with a poet's sight and sympathy.

> "I was born sickly, poor, and mean,
>   A slave; no misery could screen
>   The holders of the pearl of price
>   From Cæsar's envy; therefore twice
>   I fought with beasts, and three times saw
>   My children suffer by his law;
>   At last my own release was earned;
>   I was some time in being burned,
>   But at the close a hand came through
>   The fire above my head, and drew
>   My soul to Christ, whom now I see.
>   Sergius, a brother, writes for me
>   This testimony on the wall;
>   For me, I have forgot it all."

II.

ADVANCEMENT IN RELIGION.

CONCERNING advancement in religion, I have learned three lessons from the story of the Magi seeking the infant Christ.

First, God is true to his own word. His word is something you can rest on, as men may stand on granite.

It is in one of what are called the minor prophets, that the prediction of the birth of Christ is to be found. The prophetic word was uttered seven hundred years before the birth took place. God did not forget that word. Christ was born in Bethlehem. More than that — the mightiest earthly power was laid under tribute, that this word might be kept to the last letter. Mary the virgin was at Nazareth, a village of Galilee; but she was brought to Bethlehem in Judæa, and there the Lord was born. And how? Cæsar Augustus was a link in the chain of that fulfilment. He issued a decree of universal taxing. The decree compelled the visit of Mary thither. Even Augustus, on the world's topmost throne, must lend his aid, though all unwittingly, to the accurate keeping of the divine promise. God's word is a sure word.

Now it is right to reason from a certainty of the divine word here, to the certainty of it in other places. When God says that "unto the upright there ariseth light in the darkness"; when we are told that "he that is willing to do his will, shall know of the doctrine"; we may be certain that behind such utterances as well, there is the unchangeable veracity of God. If we but yield our hearts and lives to such divine direction, we must get on into the shining. He who so carefully kept that word concerning the birth of Jesus, will keep also his other words.

This is the second lesson: Advancement in religion is not altogether dependent upon external advantages. We would say that the likeliest man in all Judæa to find the Lord would be Herod, the king. He need take no long journey as the Magi must. He was in Jerusalem, and Bethlehem was but six miles distant. Before him were the Scriptures, pointing, through all their prophecy, to this great advent. Besides, he could consult learned doctors of the law, who knew concerning what they spake. Herod held all possible advantages in his grasp, and yet Herod did not find Jesus. The Magi found him. External advantages are not needful to advancement in religion. People often think they are. How many times they say, "If I were but a person of more leisure; if only I were not driven quite so much by work; if I were not tangled in such perplexities, or burdened with such duties; if I were a minister; if I had an hour now and then for retirement and meditation; then I might get on into the shining. But it is impossible to expect one like me to do it. From Monday morning to Saturday night I am driven as balls are from a cannon. I have hardly time to pray — scarcely time to think. Everything is against me. Other men can be religious, I cannot." But Herod held affluent advantage in his hand, and did not find the Lord. The Magi found him. It is not on what we call external advantage that advancement in religion hangs.

This is the third lesson: On what then does progress into the shining depend? Here is the answer, "Unto the upright there ariseth light in the darkness." This uprightness involves resolute setting of one's soul toward the light vouchsafed; that is to say, we need absolute and utter self-surrender to the light we have. See these Magi. They came from the East, five months' journey from Jerusalem, following the shining in the sky, hoping it to be the augury of the Messiah. They saw that light and yielded themselves to it. And though the radiance passed out of the heavens for a time, still they surrendered themselves to its memory, and went on whither it had seemed to point. Through all that five months' journey, over desert places and along rough and rocky ways, they followed the gleaming, surrendering to it, and using the light they had. From Jerusalem they went forth to Bethlehem, and then again the light shone out; and this added light they used, utterly determined and utterly sincere, with faces set toward the finding of the promised Christ. "Unto the upright there ariseth light in the darkness." To those who, following the light they have, thus go on in using it, the dimmer light shall pass into a brighter, and that into a light more radiant still, until, at last, they, with the Magi, fall before the very presence of the Lord.

III.

THE SIGHT WHICH SATISFIES.

HERE is an eagle yonder, holding himself on pinions almost motionless a mile or more above the surface of the earth. But his prey is on the earth and not in the air, and from that distance he must be able to see his prey distinctly — squirrel, rabbit, chicken, fish. But as he swoops down to seize his prey it is needful that he be able to see it with similar distinctness at close range, or, coming into nearness with it, he will miss it. Having such a power of flight, the eagle's need is at once a telescopic and a microscopic vision. Well, the eagle's need is perfectly supplied. What is not true of your eye or mine is true of the eye of the eagle. The ball of his eye is surrounded by fifteen little plates — sclerotic bones. They form a kind of ring around the eye, and their edges slightly overlap. When the eagle looks at a distant object, this little circle of bones expands, and the ball of the eye, relieved from pressure, becomes flatter; when he looks at a near object the little bones press together and the ball of the eye is squeezed into a more convex shape. Who is the near-sighted person? The one with round eyeballs. Who is the far-sighted person? The one with flatter eyeballs. But the eagle, by these sclerotic bones, can make his eye round to see near to, or flat to see far off, at will. Thus the need of varying vision, springing out of his ability of vast and varying flight, is met. There is adjustment and adaptation between need and supply.

And this instance is but a specimen; this great law of supply over against need strikes through all realms. And it rules in the topmost realm of man's spiritual nature also. You will remember how at the last passover our Lord celebrated, certain Greeks came saying, "We would see Jesus." Whether they knew it or not, they really were but prophecies and illustrations of multitudes turning with spiritual need toward the supply for it. Think a little of this fact of supply in Jesus for need, vast and hungry, in man's spiritual nature. Mating himself with this great fact and law of need and supply for need striking through all realms, Jesus stands, for man's spiritual nature, the sight which satisfies.

Well, man is craving for certainty of the divine sympathy; not always, perhaps, when, as he does now and then, he feels sufficient for himself under blue skies and with smooth ways beneath his feet; but always, however, in the greater crises of his life. And it is singular how little of this certainty of a divine sympathy he can wrest from nature. I went once to see one who was in trouble long and sore. It was in the beautiful spring weather, and there was a tender gleam on everything. But the very beauty and brightness all around seemed to be a kind of affront to this poor heart. Nature was in another, and, as it seemed to her, unfeeling mood. "I do not see how the sun can shine on so," she said, "when I am in such misery." I think we have all seen seasons which can furnish interpretation to such moods. The brightness of nature wore the look of a hard carelessness of our sadness. I read once of a poor fellow wounded in one of the battles of the war, lying on the battle-field in his own pain and amid all the death and horror about him, looking up toward the moon and the brighter stars the moonbeams did not put out, and wondering why both moon and stars did not shed sorrowing rays as they looked down on such a spectacle. I think the loneliest sight I have ever seen is that of the

fishermen's little boats amid the great wide sea
as the ocean steamer has ploughed her way
across the banks of Newfoundland. The boats
so small, the sea so great! And when the fogs
drop, as they often do, and the waves dash, and
the fishermen get lost upon the awful sea, there
is no expression of care or sympathy for them in
the blinding fog and in the driving sea. I think
every now and then a man seems to himself to
be in such a case. And he can find no sympathy in nature. And, just as truly, there is for
him a failing and not-far-enough-reaching sympathy in friends. Have you never gone in some
deep trouble of catastrophe or momentous decision to some friend, and come away with the
consciousness that, after all, you had got to
bear your own burden, make your own decision,
stand your own pain? You wanted something
from your friend you did not get, and could not.

But how full of an interpreting and trouble-
reaching sympathy is Jesus Christ! He touched
whom no one else would touch—the leper.
He noticed at once the finger of faith upon the
far fringes of his mantle amid the thronging of
the crowd. He wept at the grave of Lazarus,
though one would think his provision of the
mighty miracle he was just about to work
would have dried tears as the sun dries the

early summer dew. In certain moods there is nothing so precious to me as the study of the exquisite and tender disclosures of sympathy in Jesus. And Jesus Christ is the disclosure of the heart of God. No man hath seen God at any time; the only begotten Son which is in the bosom of the Father, he hath declared him, that is, disclosed him.

Do you remember that pathetic scene in the upper room at Jerusalem? The disciples knew they were confronting a great trouble, and as they entered it they wanted to know about God and have the consciousness of his sympathy with them in it. "Show us the Father; that sufficeth us," was their cry. And Jesus pointed them to neither sun nor stars nor flowers, not toward nature, but toward himself, and said: "He that hath seen me hath seen the Father." So, if you would know God, you must look to Jesus, and sight of him is sight of the divine sympathy. Gazing at him, you cannot but be sure God cares. Make him your confessional, till in his heart all your troubles rest. Well, when sometimes I have done it there has come a peace and rest so unique and heart-filling I was more sure than I was of anything that God did hear and care.

Another crying craving in man's heart is for

knowledge of future destiny. What an atrocious
article that was by Colonel Ingersoll on suicide!
Ah, me, what cold comfort there is, at best, in
infidelity! I have been thinking a good deal
about it lately in contrast with the comfort
which Christ gives. I have been waiting, every
day or so, beside the bed of an aged saint. Her
life is pretty much behind her — its toils, cares,
heroisms. It cannot be long before the final
summons shall reach her. What could infidelity
say to her? Really nothing more than this:
" Well, your life is finished; as to any other
and better life we can know nothing; it is all a
guess at best. If, in your age and feebleness,
you should want to end things — well, we would
not dissuade you from the step; suppose you try
it; we can promise you nothing more or other
than the possibility of doing that." O, the
hard, cold heartlessness of infidelity! I have
been flooded with a whelming thankfulness as I
have thought of what Jesus has given me to-day.
I have bidden the aged saint fix the eye of her
faith on him. I have said over to her the words
of Jesus: " Let not your heart be troubled; in
my Father's house are many mansions; I will
come and receive you to myself." And, as I
have marked the satisfaction which Jesus gives
in such an hour, I have said over and over again

to myself, " It is the sight of Jesus which meets and fills the sorest need ; thank God for the good news of heaven and eternal health and undimmed triumph which Jesus brings." Yes, the sight of Jesus is the sight which satisfies. In him there is fulness of supply over against our most crying needs.

" We would see Jesus — this is all we're needing,
    Strength, joy, and willingness come with the sight ;
We would see Jesus, dying, risen, pleading,
    Then welcome day, and farewell mortal night ! "

IV.

THE DIVINE THOUGHT OF US.

SINGS the Psalmist in the one hundred and thirty-ninth Psalm: "How precious are thy thoughts unto me, O God!" That is, toward me, the Psalmist's meaning being that loving thoughts from God are running out continually and specifically toward himself. It is a difficult faith for us sometimes, I grant, that God has precious thoughts toward us; that God personally thinks of each personal one of us.

The mass and massiveness of the universe sometimes makes the faith difficult. Among the million worlds above you, you can find no star upon which your thought alighting can fold her wing and say, This is the limit of creation; beyond, is emptiness. And all below you, on leaves, in dew-drops, within the least boundaries you can get conception of, you discover the same wealth of creative skill. And when one sends his thought down the long line of life beneath him, and then bids it climb the interminable ascent of life above him, beyond worlds, through cherubim, seraphim, principalities, powers, till the poor thought reels and sinks — how easy and despairing the confession, O, in the mind of Him upon whose arm all these are hanging, there can be no room for any special thought of me !

The inexorability of law, also, sometimes makes it difficult for us to be steadfast in the faith that God personally thinks of every one of us. Law is very real and stern, and even crushing. If law rule so resolutely, where can there be any room or use for special divine thought of me ? We sometimes ask despairingly, Is not the world, after all, but a vast machine given over into the grip of law, till the machine run down and wear out ?

The consciousness in sin, also, makes difficult the faith in God's special thought of each of us. Sin is separation. Impurity cannot dwell with purity. We are sure of that — and we are impure. And so there comes often into our sinful hearts a feeling of orphanage ; and we wonder whether, because of sin, God has not ceased thought of us.

So sometimes, amid a great and torturing trouble, we lose faith in the special thought of

God about us. We say, — often, in sore trouble, we cannot help saying it, — If God really and particularly think of me, how can such buffeting trouble come to me?

But still it is fact, God does think of us. Still it is the most right thing and reasonable for us to say with the Psalmist: " How precious are thy thoughts unto me, O God! How great is the sum of them!"

Because of the particularity of the divine knowledge, we have right to faith in God's special thought of each of us. It is the infirmity of a human and finite knowledge that it must always be, to a greater or less extent, a knowledge merely general and at the surface; it must content itself largely with the mere appearances of things. Here is a solid cube. I may learn *about* it — its hardness, its density, its shape, its thickness, its weight. But after I have learned all this, I must be still ignorant of the constituent elements of that cube. I cannot go down into the heart of it, and tell what are its ultimate atoms.

And so the organization of our knowledge, the classifying it into genera and species, proceeds rather upon our ignorance than upon what we really know. The word " tree " stands in our minds to represent the great class of trees. But we throw all trees into this great class, not because we intimately know each tree, not because we have ever seen or can ever see a millionth part of all the trees that are, but simply because we suppose all trees to bear some general resemblance to each other; and so, when we think of the class tree, we think, in a very vague and general way, not of specific trees, but of vast numbers of them thrown into the great tree-class. But such knowledge is not accurate or specific; it deals more with classes than with individuals; with generals than with particulars.

But with God the case is very different. He creates all things; therefore he must know all things utterly. There must be, in the divine mind, a separate thought of each separate thing, since he creates each separate thing. So the divine knowledge cannot be bounded by the mere appearance, by the outside; it must pierce to the hidden essence. Since God created me, he must utterly, thoroughly, separately, distinctly *know* me. He must have thought of me. Creation compels personal and distinct thought about the thing or being created. This sort of specific knowledge comes out wonderfully in this Psalm:

"I will praise thee, for I am fearfully and wonderfully made; marvellous are thy works; and that my soul knoweth right well. My substance was not hid from thee when I was made in secret, and curiously wrought in the lowest parts of the earth. Thine eyes did see my substance, yet being unperfect; and in thy book all my members were written, which in continuance were fashioned, when as yet there was none of them."

But besides, we have right to faith in the specializing divine thought of us, because such personal thought of separate persons is so continually illustrated in the life of our Lord Jesus. Christ is the grandest and surest reason for faith. I may surmise the day is dawning when I see the glimmer of the morning twilight. I am sure the day has come when the sun bursts through the radiant gates. So I may gain reason for my faith from various sources, and, therefore quite confidently hope some blissful truth is real. But tremor is changed to tremorlessness when the truth shines from the face of the Lord Jesus.

The Being who walked that sorrowful path through Galilee and Samaria and Judæa was distinguished by no more noticeable peculiarity than this: a minutely personal thought about the men and women around him, whether they were Pharisee or Sadducee, Hebrew or Samaritan, bond or free, centurion or servant. Our Lord Jesus was no respecter of persons in his thoughtful sympathy. Take but a single case of multitudes. Blindness had shrouded one from babyhood. Through the power of Jesus the waters of Siloam had washed away his lifetime darkness. "Who opened thine eyes?" asked the Pharisees. With the new light filling his eyeballs the man told of Him who was called Jesus. Then Pharisaic bigotry sought to dim the glory of the sight-giver. Then the brave, joyful heart of the man protested in sure testimony, and would not have it so. Then they cast him out of the synagogue. And so he wandered forth, with the blight of excommunication on him, disowned of parents, avoided by his friends. But he could not wander away from the thought of Jesus. Though the world turned against him, Jesus would turn toward him. Jesus sought him, Jesus found him — the poor, exiled, friendless man, to warm him with his sympathy, to embrace him with his love, to bless him with his forgiveness.

I am sure the argument is legitimate. O Christ, thou art the express image of the Godhead bodily! O Christ, thou art always the same Christ. O Christ, as thou didst think about and seek for the man born blind, so in all trial and loneliness, thou wilt think of me. Yea, verily, since Christ has come and lived

before me I may be sure that God does think
of me.   I have right to rejoice in the sweet
music of this psalm.   Listen how it sings to us
of God's particularizing thought of us : —

"O Lord, thou hast searched me and known me.
Thou knowest my downsitting and my uprising; thou
understandest my thought afar off.   Thou compassest
my path and my lying down, and art acquainted with
all my ways.   Thou hast beset me behind and before,
and laid thine hand upon me."

So I gladly make answer and say, As thy
thoughts toward me are precious, O my God, so
is my thought of thy thought, precious.

It is precious for *work*.   Work is difficult,
sometimes tasking, straining.   Often, too, work
seems barren of result, as though one into desert
sands were casting seeds.   Frequently, as well,
the work set against our hands seems service
small, inconspicuous, almost worthless.   But if
God think of me ; if he knows my place of work
and sort of work, and my frequent weariness
amidst it ; if he knows I *try* to serve him and to
please him ; if he regards my motive, though
to my eye such slight result appears — why, then
the lowliest and the hardest toil is a pleasure
and delight.   And God does know, does take
account of motive.   One tells how he saw " in

the private treasury of Windsor Castle, a great gold peacock sparkling with rubies, emeralds, and diamonds, which had been brought away from some rajah's palace; and close by it a common quill pen, and a bit of serge discolored. The pen had signed some important treaty; the bit of serge was the fragment of a flag that had waved over some hard-fought field. The two together were worth a halfpenny, but they held their ground beside the jewels; for they meant successful effort and heroic devotion for the interests of the kingdom, and therefore were laid up in the treasure-house of the king." "So is it," this narrator goes on to say, "with our poor work. Its worth depends on motive." Yes, working out of the motive of pleasing God, of doing his will, I may be sure God thinks upon my work, somehow uses it, deeply treasures it, builds it into the purposes of his great grace.

Also, my thought of God's thought of me is precious for *trial.* Beneficent are the trials of God's thoughtful sending. They are not punitive; they are educative. And he knows just what trial and how much I need.

Also, my thought of God's thought of me is precious for *guard.* If I were but the sport of law, if I were only the issue of a dead and heartless mechanism, then I might, with reason, say to myself, " There is no such thing as difference between right and wrong ; moral discriminations are but myths ; I will live lawlessly, and charge the blame of it, if there can be blame, to heredity and environment." But God thinks upon me. Then all ground is holy. Let me then, wherever I may be, refuse sin, enduring as seeing Him who is invisible.

> " Dear Lord, my heart shall no more doubt
>   That thou dost compass me about
>   With sympathy divine.
>   The Love for me once crucified
>   Is not the love to leave my side,
>   But waiteth ever to divide
>   Each smallest care of mine."

V.

TRUTH TO ONE'S SELF.

WHEN David went out to fight Goliath, he would not go as a mailed warrior. He would not pretend to be what he was not. He was shepherd — nothing more. Thus his weapons weré not Saul's sword and shield. They were the sling and stone. He would go forth as shepherd with his sling and stone. He would not go otherwise. He would be true to himself.

It is not always so with men. It is always so in nature. Things are true to themselves. Seeds will never cheat you — though seed-merchants sometimes will. Wheat is always wheat. When you sow wheat, you will reap wheat harvests. I have ridden out over the prairies of the Northwest; wild oats produce wild oats alone. A rose bears roses. A tulip-bulb will not build a pyramid of hyacinths. An oak never forgets itself and changes into a maple or a thistle. The wonder of my boyhood was an old pear-tree in the back yard that used to bear each season seven different kinds of pears. It was a common pear-tree, hanging out in its natural condition a very common and worthless sort of fruit. But there had been grafted into the various branches of it other and more valuable varieties. The trunk was just the same; the roots were just the same; and the roots went down, reaching amid the soil for the usual nourishment, out of which the tree was to manufacture its comparatively poor fruitage. But when, in the springtime, the sap began to climb the trunk, and flow out along the branches, and touch these slips which had been inserted in them, then these ingrafted slips could not become unmindful of their higher destiny. Out of that same sap they must elaborate pears of exactly the same variety to which they themselves belonged. And so, because each ingrafted slip could not be other than true to itself, the autumn crown of the old tree was manifold.

This is a deep principle for life — truth to one's self. He is not the best man who imitates most exactly. He is the best man who is most thoroughly himself. Only let him be sure that he is in righteousness and purity. Well-being is the root of well-doing. Then, having received the new birth and the righteousness which Christ gives, let the man, in truth to himself, work out his own nature and capacity. So shall he illustrate God's meaning in his life. So shall he dwell in the sunshine of sincerity.

VI.

A GOOD MEDICINE.

 MERRY heart is a good medicine — as the Revised Version translates the proverb. Yes, a merry — that is, a shining, cheerful, thankful — heart *is* a good medicine.

It is the within which makes mainly the without. Special observations to determine the duration of sunshine in Europe have been taken. It was found that while Spain has the most sunshine, Scotland has the least. But what of the inner sunshine of head and heart which is the real source of the national life? Spain, with its bigotries, priestcraft, cruelties, illiteracies, feeblenesses, has the least of this; Scotland, with all its mists, clouds, rains, has of the shining of this " sun behind the sun " the most. You remember the true melodious lines of Coleridge, —

" Ah, from the soul itself must issue forth
A light, a glory, a fair, luminous cloud
Enveloping the earth —

And from the soul itself must there be sent
A sweet and potent voice, of its own birth,
Of all sweet sounds the life and element!
We in ourselves rejoice!
And thence flows all that charms or ear or sight,
All melodies the echoes of that voice,
All colors a suffusion of that light."

Well, a merry heart will cure the ill of looking at the darker side of things. There in England, where the land ends, and the foot of the island pushes itself far out into the sea, you come upon a house. Approaching the house from one side, you read, written on its walls, the legend, " This is the last house in England " — and that is melancholy enough. But, passing around the house, and approaching it from its other side, you read this legend, written on its other wall, " This is the first house in England " — and the whole prospect brightens. It is the merry heart which has steady eyes for the brighter side.

Also, a merry heart will cure laggard work. " Father, what is an optimist ? " the boy asked. The father thought a little, and then said, " Now, sonny, you know I can't give ye the dictionary meanin' of that word, no more'n I can of a great many others. But I've got a kind of an idee what it means. Probably you

don't remember your Uncle Henry, but I guess
if there ever was an optimist he was one.
Things was always comin' out right with
Henry, and especially anything hard that he
had to do; it wa'n't a-goin' to be hard — 'twas
jist kind of solid pleasant. Take hoein' corn,
now. If anything kind of took the tucker out
of me, 'twas hoein' corn in the hot sun. But
in the field, long about the time I begun to lag
back a little, he'd look up an' say, ' Good, Jim!
When we get these two rows hoed, an' eighteen
more, the piece'll be half done!' An' he'd say
it in such a kind of a cheerful way that I
couldn't 'a' ben any more tickled if the piece
had been all done — an' the rest would go light
enough." Anybody can see, if a man goes at
his work with a heart like that, whether his
work be hoeing corn, or merchandising, or
school teaching, or clerking, or carpentering,
or preaching, his work will be swiftly and well
done.

Also, a sunny heart will cure the ill of useless
discipline. This is a probationary world. This
is a world in which we are getting ready for
another, infinitely larger, infinitely nobler. And
discipline must be a necessarily constituent element in the process of getting ready for that
better world. And it makes all the difference

in the world how you take the discipline, whether it be blight or blessing to you; whether it be use-*ful* or use-*less*.   But a merry heart — that is, a strong, brave, thoughtful, shining heart — is a sort of medicine which will prevent discipline from becoming useless, hardening.

There are some medicines which, if you may trust the advertisements of them, are even universal medicines.   Meet every ill — neuralgia, stomach-ache, rheumatism, heart-disease, consumption, worms, whooping - cough, measles, mumps — with this medicine, and, according to the advertisement, you vanquish it.   But, after all, when you come to think of it, is not this good medicine of a sunny heart a really quite universal remedy?

But where and how can you get this medicine of a sunny heart?   Well, you may get and take this good medicine of a sunny heart by taking short views.   Mr. T. W. Higginson tells of a little boy who one night roused his mother by a violent fit of weeping.   When she went to his bed to find the cause of a grief so deep and strong, the little fellow sobbed out, " I'm afraid — when I grow up — that I sha' n't have money enough — to pay my taxes."

But there are older people quite as unwise

as the little boy. They forebode; they conjure up all sorts of shapes of ills in the far future. They borrow trouble. They load themselves down needlessly in preparation for that altogether imagined and conjured up contingency. I have read of a certain high Chinese official, despatched on a special errand, who gave orders that a hundred and fifty pounds of salt should be placed in his luggage, lest he should find no salt in the European country whither he was going. There are multitudes of foreboding people who weight themselves just as unwisely. It is impossible that they have a merry heart. They are strained, anxious, burdened. Such can get this good medicine of a merry heart by taking short views.

Also, we may get and take this good medicine of a merry heart by counting mercies. " It ain't so hard to be contented with the things we have," said the old woman dolefully; " it's being contented with the things we have n't that's so tryin'." " I don't know about that," said Uncle Silas; " when we begin to look at the things our neighbors have and we have n't, we always pick out just the things we want. They live in a nice house, we say, and we have only a little one. They have money.

and we need to count every penny. They have an easy time, and we have to work. We never say: 'They had the typhoid fever, but it did not come near us. They have a son in the insane asylum, but our brains are sound. Staggering feet go into their grand door, but nothing worse than tired ones come home to ours at night.' You see when we begin to call Providence to account for the things that don't come to us, it's only fair to take in all kinds of things."

Count your individual mercies. There was a dear, serene old lady. Somehow a sweet and beautiful light kept falling on her face. The lines of care and irritation could not be found in it. A woman given to fretfulness and almost annoyed at such steady placidity, asked her the secret of her content. "My dear, I keep a pleasure book," she said. Speech went on about it, and at last the pleasure book was shown. It was filled with items like these: " Saw a beautiful lily in a window." " Talked to a bright, happy girl." " Received a kind letter from a dear friend." " Enjoyed a beautiful sunset." " Husband brought some roses home to me." " My boy out to-day for the first time after the croup." " Have you found pleasure for every day?" wistfully asked the fretful woman. " Yes, for every day, even the sad ones," was the low-toned answer. Ah, yes, keep you a pleasure book; count you your mercies; so you can get and take this good medicine of a merry heart.

But after all, the best way to get and take this good medicine of a merry heart is by the cherishing of a steady faith in God. I have read how Pastor Herne carved over the lintel of his house the motto, " God is overhead. All's well."

THE END.

Classics of the Quiet Hour.

Each book, 25 cents. Dainty cloth bindings.

These books give the choicest thoughts from the best works of the foremost devotional writers. The complete works of these great authors are too formidable for many readers, but Dr. Clark has, with great care, selected their best thoughts, and has also written for each volume a bright introduction, giving an exceedingly helpful and interesting sketch of the author's life and works.

The Presence of God. By FRANCIS E. CLARK, D. D.
Selections from the devotional works of Bishop Jeremy Taylor.

Living and Loving. By FRANCIS E. CLARK, D. D.
Selections from the devotional works of Prof. A. Tholuck.

The Golden Alphabet. By FRANCIS E. CLARK, D. D.
Selections from the works of Master John Tauler.

The Kingdom Within. By FRANCIS E. CLARK, D. D.
Selections from "Imitation of Christ," by Thomas à Kempis.

Quaint Thoughts. By BELLE M. BRAIN. Fifty quaint selections from an old-time army chaplain, Thomas Fuller.

A very delightful book with this title has been made up by Miss Brain from the writings of that famous old army chaplain, Thomas Fuller. Coleridge said that, next to Shakespeare, Thomas Fuller excited in him "the sense and emulation of the marvellous."

UNITED SOCIETY OF CHRISTIAN ENDEAVOR.

Boston	Chicago
Tremont Temple.	155 La Salle Street.

THE SURRENDERED LIFE

Quiet Hour Meditations

BY

REV. J. WILBUR CHAPMAN, D. D.

AUTHOR OF

" And Peter," " Received Ye the Holy Ghost?" etc.

"A little book, 'THE SURRENDERED LIFE: QUIET HOUR MEDITATIONS,' by the Rev. J. W. Chapman, D. D., inculcates the lesson of thoroughgoing and loyal fellowship with Christ. That it specially addresses young people makes it the more necessary to qualify its teaching that 'it is not a good thing for one to make plans for his own life,' but rather to find God's plan for us and follow it. It is only by endeavor to find out what we can best do, and trying to do it, that we find out what God would have us to do."—*The Outlook.*

Daintily bound in cloth. Price, 50 cents, postpaid.

UNITED SOCIETY OF CHRISTIAN ENDEAVOR,

Tremont Temple,
Boston, Mass.

155 La Salle St.,
Chicago, Ills.

Recent Publications.

A Daily Message for Christian Endeavorers. By MRS. FRANCIS E. CLARK. With introduction by Dr. Clark. Beautifully illustrated. Boxed. 384 pages. Price, only $1.00.

This is a book for the Quiet Hour, the Prayer Meeting, and the Birthday. It is three books in one. There is a page for every day in the year, filled with the choicest thoughts of the best writers, that will enrich and deepen the spiritual life of every reader. The collection is the result of years of careful reading, and most of the selections will be found peculiarly appropriate for use in prayer meetings. The index of subjects will enable one to find choice quotations on almost any topic. A new feature in books of this kind is the place for birthday entries, space being given under every day in the year. The choicest gift-book of the year.

The Morning Watch. Or Thoughts for the Quiet Hour. By BELLE M. BRAIN. Cloth. Beautifully illustrated. Boxed. 414 pages. Price, $1.00.

Here are 366 diamonds of the rarest color and brilliancy, gems from the heart and brain and hand of the saints of God of all ages. With this book in your possession, you can live for a month and hold daily conversation with Andrew Murray, F. B. Meyer, A. J. Gordon, Francis E. Clark, D. L. Moody, J. R. Miller, and others. They will speak to you from the hours of their richest and deepest experience. If you want to draw near to God, you can have no better help than the daily message from his word and from his servant that this book will bring you.

The Great Secret. By REV. FRANCIS E. CLARK, D. D. Dainty cloth binding. Price, only 30 cents.

The secret of Health, Beauty, Happiness, Friend-Making, Common Sense, and Success are all explained in "The Great Secret." These articles attracted wide-spread attention as they appeared in *The Golden Rule*, and were so helpful to many that numerous requests were received for their publication in book form. The secret of life and peace and blessedness is told in such a charming and convincing way that the reader is swept along to the author's own conclusion; and, as he closes the book, says, "I, too, will 'practise the presence of God.'"

Send all orders with remittance to

UNITED SOCIETY OF CHRISTIAN ENDEAVOR

Tremont Temple, Boston, Mass.

155 La Salle St., Chicago, Ills.

CPSIA information can be obtained
at www.ICGtesting.com
Printed in the USA
BVHW091236261118
534010BV00012B/351/P